Cornerstones of Freedom

The Story of

THE ASSASSINATION OF JOHN F. KENNEDY

By R. Conrad Stein

Illustrated by Keith Neely

CHILDRENS PRESS®

CHICAGO

Library of Congress Cataloging in Publication Data

Stein, R. Conrad.
    The story of the assassination of John F. Kennedy

    (Cornerstones of freedom)
    Summary: Describes the assassination of President
Kennedy, the reactions of a stunned world, his funeral
services, and the controversy over the investigation of
the killing.
    1. Kennedy, John F. (John Fitzgerald), 1917-1963—
Assassination—Juvenile literature. [1. Kennedy,
John F. (John Fitzgerald), 1917-1963—Assassination.
2. Kennedy, John F. (John Fitzgerald), 1917-1963—
Funeral and memorial services] I. Neely, Keith,
1943-   ill. II. Title. III. Series.
E842.9.S69   1985   973.922′092′4   85-10936
ISBN 0-516-04693-4   AACR2

On a sunny November day in 1963, the plane called Air Force One landed at Love Field in Dallas, Texas. A band struck up the rousing song "Hail to the Chief." Out of the aircraft stepped the smiling president of the United States and his young and beautiful wife. The first lady wore a pink suit and a matching hat. Most of the flashing cameras were aimed at her. She received so much adoration on the Texas trip that earlier in the day the president had joked to reporters, "You remember me? I'm the guy who accompanied Jacqueline Kennedy to Texas."

Never in memory had so glamorous a figure as John Fitzgerald Kennedy occupied the White House. President Kennedy was the youngest man ever elected to the nation's highest office. He followed Dwight Eisenhower, one of the oldest chief executives to serve. The passage of power between the two was like a torch being handed to a new generation. Kennedy and his wife filled the White House with music and dance, with thinkers, poets, and rebels. Historian Bruce Catton later wrote,

"Whatever he [Kennedy] did was done with zest, as if youth were for the first time touching life and finding it exciting."

But although he was much admired, President Kennedy also had bitter enemies. He was a Roman Catholic, the first of his faith to become president. He supported the rights of black people at a time when blacks in some southern states were forbidden to enter "white" restaurants or "white" movie theaters or "white" rest rooms. He favored a treaty with Russia that ended the atmospheric testing of nuclear weapons. In 1963, his religion and his ideals were unacceptable in many regions of the country. One of those regions was Dallas, Texas. The day before his visit, an anti-Kennedy group distributed circulars that bore a large picture of the president. Below it were the words: WANTED FOR TREASON.

The crowds lining the sidewalks were friendly, however, as the presidential motorcade wound through Dallas. Many well-wishers waved their hands and shouted to the first lady. "Jackie, over here! Jackie! Here, here, here!" Mrs. Kennedy tried to wave back to all callers. In a year, the president was due to run for reelection, and winning the Texas vote was an important goal.

Since the day was so balmy, the Kennedys rode in an open convertible limousine. In the jump seats in front of them sat the governor of Texas and his wife. The crowds thinned as the big limousine approached a diamond-shaped grassy field known as Dealey Plaza. Looming above was a drab seven-story building called the Texas School Book Depository. The governor's wife turned and smiled at the president. She said, "You can't say Dallas isn't friendly to you today."

John Kennedy never answered. A crack of rifle
fire cut him down, and the world has never been the
same again.

In the presidential car, figures of people moved as
if in a slow-motion nightmare. John Kennedy's body
lurched. Governor John Connally slumped forward.
A guard assigned to protect the president leaped
onto the back of the limousine. There he grabbed

Mrs. Kennedy, who in terror had also climbed onto the back of the car. The guard pushed her back into the seat. He saw blood soaking the car seats. Frustrated and angry, he pounded on the trunk. Police sirens screamed, and the limousine sped toward a hospital with Mrs. Kennedy cradling her husband's limp body in her arms.

Moments later, a bulletin from United Press International announced to the world, THREE SHOTS WERE FIRED AT PRESIDENT KENNEDY'S MOTORCADE TODAY IN DOWNTOWN DALLAS. Within minutes, all television and radio stations reported the news. CBS television interrupted a daytime soap opera called "As the World Turns," and the famous newscaster Walter Cronkite appeared. He seemed confused and unable to believe the news bulletins being rushed to his desk. "The first reports say the president was seriously wounded," said Cronkite. Further bulletins claimed that Governor John Connally also had been hit by gunfire. Finally, official word came from Parkland Hospital in Dallas. "The president is dead," Mr. Cronkite announced. The veteran newsman then sat speechless for half a minute before he was able to continue his report.

The announcement of Kennedy's death came at 2:00 P.M. Eastern Standard Time on Friday, November 22, 1963. People who lived through that day can remember precisely where they were and what they were doing when they heard the stunning news. And they can still recall their first thoughts— *Impossible. It can't be. Not Kennedy—he's too young. Who could have done this? Poor Jackie.*

A strange silence gripped the country. Men and women who were home alone stepped outside simply because they felt a compelling need to be with others. Workers quietly walked off their jobs, and their supervisors didn't object. Teachers dismissed classes. Churches filled with worshippers. People wept openly on the streets. Arthur Schlesinger, who worked as Kennedy's assistant, recalled a friend telling him, "Now we'll never laugh again." Schlesinger answered, "Heavens—we'll laugh again. It's just that we'll never be young again."

The assassination began an incredible four-day story that was witnessed by millions of television viewers. For most of that long weekend, people all around the world did nothing but watch coverage of a story that included murder, police bungling, and an international outpouring of grief. It also included a funeral ceremony that was immensely sad, yet hauntingly beautiful. The story starred Jacqueline Kennedy, whose quiet courage will always be etched in the memory of the masses of people who watched her ordeal.

Minutes after the shooting, police scoured the buildings surrounding Dealey Plaza. One officer stopped a man who was running through the second-floor employees' lunchroom at the Texas School Book Depository. The building superintendent told the policeman, "He's okay. He works here." The officer nodded as if to say, "All right," and allowed the man to pass. The employee was twenty-four-year-old Lee Harvey Oswald. He would forever remain a dark and mysterious figure in history.

Oswald's life had been a study in failure. A high-school dropout, he enlisted in the Marine Corps, but received an undesirable discharge. He then traveled to the Soviet Union, where he proclaimed that he

was a Communist and applied for Russian citizenship. After a lengthy stay, Soviet authorities denied him citizenship, and Oswald returned to the United States with a Russian-born wife and a small baby. He bounced from job to job until he was hired as an order filler in the Texas School Book Depository building in October, 1963. His starting wage was $1.25 an hour. Evidence suggests that on the day the motorcade wound through the streets below, Oswald hid near a sixth-floor window, and fired at the president with a cheap, mail-order rifle.

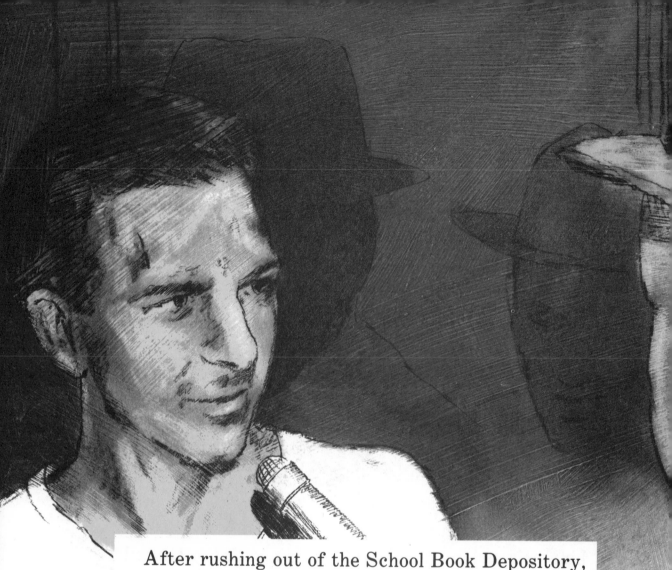

After rushing out of the School Book Depository,
Oswald boarded a bus and later a taxi to reach the
dingy rooming house in which he lived. There he put
a pistol in his jacket pocket and returned to the
streets. At his job site, his absence was noticed, and
Oswald became a suspect in the search for a gunman. His description was broadcast to all squad
cars. A Dallas patrolman named J. D. Tippit spotted
Oswald hurrying down a sidewalk and ordered him

to halt. Oswald drew his pistol and fired three times. Officer Tippit was killed instantly. Thirty-five minutes later, Oswald was seized inside a movie theater. "Everybody will know who I am now," he shouted to an arresting officer. The Dallas police told reporters they had captured a "hot suspect."

An hour after Oswald's arrest, the drama of the day shifted back to where it had started—to Love Field and the plane called Air Force One. Vice-President Lyndon Johnson deemed it essential to be sworn in as the new president without delay. He had been riding in the car behind Kennedy's at the time the fatal shots rang out. Now he stood before a woman judge who held a small black Bible. Solemnly, Johnson took the oath of office: "I will faithfully execute the office of President of the United States. . . ."

At Johnson's side stood Mrs. Jacqueline Kennedy. Earlier in the day, she had disembarked from Air Force One as the first lady. Now, in the afternoon shadows, she had returned to the aircraft as the president's widow. Her pink suit was stained with her husband's blood. A witness described her as looking "white-faced, but dry-eyed." During the swearing-in ceremony, she stood unwavering. She

was beginning to display the magnificent grace under pressure that would make her one of the most universally admired women of her times.

After the flight to Washington, Kennedy's casket was taken to rest in the White House. The Kennedy family was devastated. A family friend said he heard Kennedy's brother Robert, locked inside a room, sobbing over and over again, "Why, God, why?" Around the world, millions of people asked the same question.

Never before had the death of one man created such immediate, universal grief. French President Charles de Gaulle told a friend, "I am stunned. They are crying all over France. It is as if he were a

Frenchman, a member of their own family." Candles burned in nearly every window in Berlin, where Kennedy had once thrilled the German people by proclaiming, *"Ich bin ein Berliner"* ("I am a Berliner."). From Ireland, the Kennedy family's ancestral home, a writer claimed, "Ah, they cried the rain down that night." In rural Mexico, peasant families tore his picture out of newspapers and placed it next to their straw figures of the Lady of Guadalupe—the country's patron saint. In Central Africa, a villager walked ten miles through the bush to find an American and say, "I have lost a friend and I am so sorry."

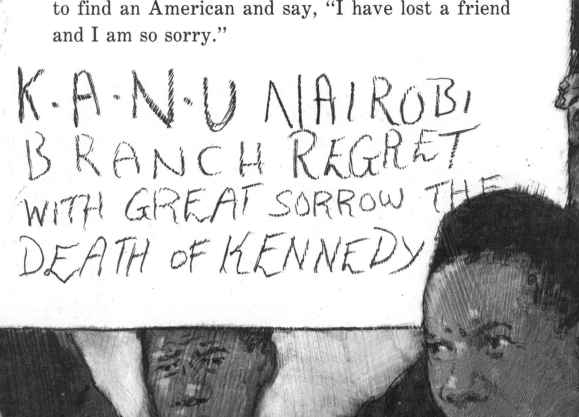

Why did the death of this American president—
who had been in office for only three years—create
such a wave of sorrow among people who lived
oceans away from the United States? Certainly it
was more than his wealth, his power, or his movie-
actor good looks. His appeal touched deeper, almost
mystical, roots. Kennedy had a remarkable ability to
reach out to people and excite them with hope. To
this day, his gift defies explanation. Ordinary men
and women perceived some sort of magic in him. So,
from the peasant in Guatemala to the businessman
in Switzerland, people mourned their loss.

Saturday, November 23, was the second day of
the four-day assassination story. A bone-chilling
rain fell on the capital and continued all day.
Funeral arrangements were made. John Kennedy
was to be buried at Arlington National Cemetery,
the resting place for military heroes. Jacqueline
Kennedy had the painful task of explaining to the
two Kennedy children that they would never see
their father again. At the time, Caroline Kennedy
was five years old and John, Jr. (called John-John
by his father) was not quite three. His birthday
would fall on Monday, the day his father was to be
buried.

In Dallas, Governor John Connally rested in a hospital bed. He had been seriously wounded in the gunfire that killed the president, but he was expected to recover. The rest of Dallas was a town in torment. Many citizens believed that the climate of hatred that had boiled in their city prior to the president's visit had encouraged the gunman. That night, dozens of families journeyed to Dealey Plaza to place flowers and floral wreaths on the grass. One flower had a note attached that was written in red crayon: "I'm sorry Caroline and John-John. Forgive us. A 9-year-old Dallas girl."

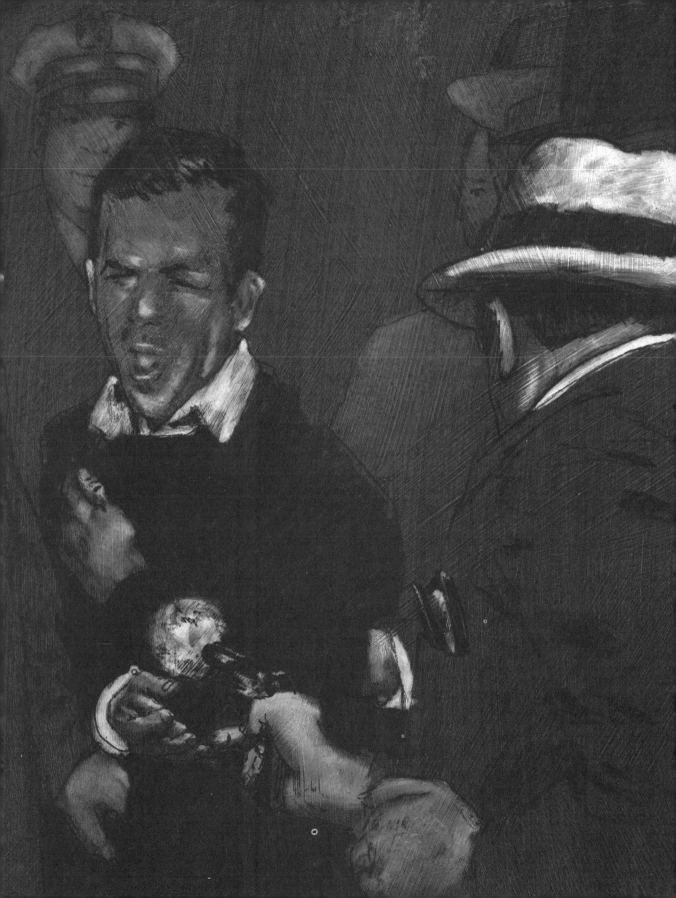

At Dallas police headquarters, newspaper reporters fumed. The biggest crime in the city's history had taken place, and the police were handling it almost as a routine case. Reporters pleaded for details on the progress of Oswald's interrogation. Police said only that so far the suspect had denied killing anyone. For reasons that were never fully explained, Oswald was questioned for less than three hours that day. Worse yet, the police kept no written transcript of the suspect's testimony.

But the Dallas Police Department's most outrageous performance would come the next day.

On Sunday, November 24, the third day of the assassination story, television crews in Washington, D.C., broadcast a Catholic High Mass. Shortly after the Mass, television stations shifted to Dallas, where Lee Harvey Oswald was to be routinely transferred to another jail facility. Through the crowded basement of the city prison, the accused gunman walked with a detective holding each arm. Suddenly, a burly man burst through the throng of policemen and reporters. He shouted, "You killed the president, you rat!" Then he shoved a pistol into Oswald's stomach and fired. This bizarre scene took place while millions of amazed viewers watched.

Two hours later, Lee Harvey Oswald died at Parkland Hospital. Ironically, this was the same hospital where Kennedy was pronounced dead, and some of the same doctors and nurses were in attendance. Oswald's slayer was a Dallas tavern owner named Jack Ruby. Because he was a familiar figure at police headquarters, Ruby had managed to slip into the prison basement. This appalling breach of security will always be a black mark in the annals of the Dallas police force. Ruby later claimed that he had become temporarily insane in his grief over the president's death and that his killing of Oswald was an act of wild impulse.

In Washington, the process of burying the president continued. A black, horse-drawn caisson bearing the president's coffin rolled down Pennsylvania Avenue from the White House toward the Capitol Building. Thousands of people lined the route, yet the silence was profound. In the Capitol Rotunda, three eulogies (speeches honoring a dead person) were given. The most powerful eulogy was delivered by Senator Mike Mansfield: "There was a father with a little boy, a little girl, and a joy of each in the other. In a moment it was no more. . . .There was a husband who asked much and gave much, and out of

the giving and the asking wove with a woman what
could not be broken in life, and in a moment it was no
more."

During the ceremonies, television cameras were
trained primarily on Jacqueline Kennedy. She shed
no tears. Her steps never faltered. Her dignity was
majestic. When the last eulogy had been delivered,
Mrs. Kennedy, with five-year-old Caroline in hand,
stepped forward and knelt in front of the flag-
draped coffin. After a silent prayer, she kissed the
flag. A reporter described the scene: "All the time
the eyes of television had been watching. They were
still watching as a beautiful and brave woman and
her little daughter walked out into the world again."

The next day, Monday, November 25, was the fourth and final day of the assassination story. It was the saddest day, for the numbness of the sudden death had worn off and people now came to the stark realization that their president would take his final journey through the streets of Washington. From every part of the globe came kings and queens, presidents, prime ministers, and tribal chiefs to walk the last mile with the Kennedy family.

The horse-drawn caisson left Capitol Hill at 11:00 A.M. Once more, thousands of people lined the street, but the only sounds came from hooves clopping on pavement and a solemn throb of drums. In the procession, a young soldier led a riderless horse to symbolize a country that had lost a leader. Behind the caisson walked Jacqueline with the two Kennedy brothers—Robert and Edward. Behind the family marched the captains and kings of the world.

It seemed that the great throngs of people who lined the route saw only Jacqueline Kennedy. The young widow, dressed in black, wore her grief like a brave flag. One reporter said, "Jacqueline Kennedy walked with a poise and grace that words cannot convey—as regal as any emperor, queen, or prince who followed her." A college president who knew the Kennedy family wrote, "Not one of us would have blamed her if she had hidden at home. Not one of us would have blamed her if she had worn dark glasses, or if she had left the children behind. Yet she went from triumph to triumph showing something for which. . .we can all be proud."

A final Mass was held at St. Matthew's Church. Surveys show that in 93 percent of all homes, Americans gathered around their television sets to watch. The Los Angeles freeways were almost empty. The Chicago Loop was deserted. Midtown Manhattan resembled the inside of a vacant cathedral. Airplanes waited at runways while pilots, crews, and passengers paused to view the proceedings in Washington.

After the Mass, the honor guard carried the coffin down the church steps, and the band played "Hail to the Chief." Then the viewing public was treated to a

picture they would remember for a lifetime. As the casket passed the Kennedy family, Jacqueline leaned over and whispered something in John-John's ear. Kennedy's son—three years old that day—raised his right hand and saluted smartly.

At Arlington National Cemetery, the honor guard removed the flag from the coffin, folded it carefully, and presented it to Mrs. Kennedy. The president was buried to the lonesome lament of a bugle sounding "Taps." The four grim days of the assassination story ended. In the words of White House correspondent Merriman Smith, "America buried John Fitzgerald Kennedy on Arlington's green slopes today, consigning his body to the land he loved and his soul to the God he worshipped. . . ."

In the days after the funeral, a host of questions burned in the minds of most Americans. Did Oswald really shoot Kennedy? If so, why? Were two, three, or four shots fired? Was there a second gunman? Finally, were the true reasons for the assassination forever lost with the death of Lee Harvey Oswald?

Hoping to provide answers to these questions, President Johnson appointed a commission headed by the chief justice of the Supreme Court, Earl Warren, to determine the truth "as far as it can be discovered." The Warren Commission conducted an intensive ten-month investigation. It took testimony from 552 witnesses, and its findings filled twenty-six books covering thousands of pages. The report of the Warren Commission concluded that Lee Harvey Oswald murdered the president, and that he acted alone when doing so.

The Warren Report came under fire soon after its publication. By the late 1960s, dozens of books had appeared, each insisting that Kennedy had been killed not by a lone gunman, but by one sinister con-

spiracy or another. Many of the writers were char-
latans who simply hoped to cash in on the public's
eagerness to read anything about Kennedy. But
some raised serious doubts as to whether Oswald
could have acted alone. They pointed out that some
eyewitnesses heard gunfire coming from the grassy
knoll in front of the presidential car, and not from
the Texas School Book Depository Building to the
rear. The writers also claimed that Oswald had been
only a mediocre marksman while in the Marine
Corps, and that his cheap rifle was too inaccurate to
score such precise hits.

In the years following Kennedy's death, attacks
on the Warren Report never ceased. In 1979, Congress appointed a new commission to study the
assassination. It concluded that Kennedy was "pro-
bably assassinated as the result of a conspiracy."
The commission speculated that Oswald was one of
the gunmen, and suggested that the organized crime
syndicate could have been involved. In a special edi-
tion to commemorate the twentieth anniversary of
the assassination, *Newsweek* magazine said, "The
judgment of the Warren Commission that Lee
Harvey Oswald alone killed Kennedy has stood up to
considerable battling over nineteen years, but hard-

ly anyone believes it any more." No conspiracy theory, however, has ever been proved absolutely.

Since the Kennedy tragedy, American public figures have lived under the shadow of the gun. Assassins have murdered Robert Kennedy, Martin Luther King, Medgar Evers, and Malcolm X. Gerald Ford was fired upon, and Ronald Reagan was seriously wounded. A gunman's bullet left Alabama's Governor George Wallace in a wheelchair. No one knows why these assassinations and assassination attempts now come with such frightening regularity. Some Americans attribute such killings and attempted killings to a general moral and spiritual decline that began with the fall of John F. Kennedy.

A year after the country buried John Kennedy, the Democratic National Convention met in Atlantic City, New Jersey. Had he lived, the convention would certainly have nominated John F. Kennedy to be its candidate for a second term. Instead, the convention named Lyndon Johnson to lead the party. But the memory of the fallen president lingered in the minds of all the delegates. The highlight of the convention came when Robert Kennedy was called upon to introduce a film about his brother's life.

After his speech, the delegates cheered for twenty-two minutes, and many were unable to hold back tears. To memorialize his brother, Robert Kennedy chose to recite these lines from Shakespeare's *Romeo and Juliet:*

When he shall die,
Take him and cut him out in little stars,
And he will make the face of heaven so fine
That all the world will be in love with night
And pay no worship to the garish sun.

About the Author

R. Conrad Stein was born and grew up in Chicago. He served in the Marine Corps and later attended the University of Illinois, where he received a Bachelor of Arts degree in history. He later studied in Mexico and earned a Master of Fine Arts degree from the University of Guanajuato.

Like many young people in the early 1960s, Mr. Stein was an admirer of President John F. Kennedy. On the morning of November 22, 1963, he was a college student studying for an exam, when his roommate burst through the door and cried out, "Did you hear? The President's been shot!" Mr. Stein will never forget the impact of Kennedy's death, nor will anyone else who lived through the haunting four days of the assassination story.

About the Artist

Keith Neely attended the School of the Art Institute of Chicago and received a Bachelor of Fine Arts degree with honors from the Art Center College of Design where he majored in illustration. He has worked as an art director, designer, and illustrator and has taught advertising illustration and advertising design at Biola College in La Mirada, California. Mr. Neely is currently a freelance illustrator whose work has appeared in numerous magazines, books, and advertisements. He lives with his wife and five children in Florida.